DEMYSTIFICATIONS

ALSO BY MIRANDA MELLIS

The Revisionist

Il Revisionista

Materialisms (chapbook)

None of This Is Real

The Spokes

The Quarry (chapbook)

The Instead

DEMYSTIFICATIONS

MIRANDA MELLIS

SOLID OBJECTS
NEW YORK

Printed in the United States of America

Design by HR Hegnauer and Jordan Wannemacher

Visual index by Katie Aymar

ISBN: 978-0-9862355-4-2

Library of Congress Control Number: 2020950714

SOLID OBJECTS
New York

The infinite multiplication of activities,
things, and vulgar names is . . .
the accomplishment of a
spiritual task of redemption.

JACQUES RANCIÈRE

How can something add up, when it is only conceived
and then understood in reverse?
By subtracting, until a lot of it is gone.

FANNY HOWE

1.

Getting up early is the cause of a long day.

2.

She didn't know what was about to be said.
She had to find out after it came out.

She knew what was about to be said.
Was she hearing faster?

How can you hear in advance?

Hearing what hasn't yet been said.
Hearing what's already been said.

All the particles of the personal mind,
finally shown to be a crowd of strangers

all deluded thus, dropped into
a silent starless garden.

3.

What happened to that giant building? Why is it empty,
its walls soft and green?

It's turned back into a forest.

After that, they never could think of architecture
without thinking of water.

4.

After the landslide, a sheer wall of dirt, flat and
punctuated by stones.

I refuse to attribute my sudden and unwelcome feelings
to anything at all.

5.

Ambition rushes up as fuel. Happiness depletes it.

Vaulting ambition, which o'erleaps itself
And falls on th'other.

6.

The trees slide uphill, greenly
layered and lineated.

Go back to your roots.

7.

We can't congratulate you on your success,
it's the first time we've heard from you in two years.

Write with bad news first.

Then we might be more receptive.

8.

Wear a suit: dressing for politics is not magical thinking.

Then it's your fault for wearing ribbons in your hair on Election Day.

You confused poll with Maypole.

You'll wear your dunce cap to the voting booth from now on!

9.

William Carlos Williams wrote

War is the first and only thing in the world today. The arts generally are not, nor is this writing a diversion from that for relief, a turning away. It is the war or part of it, merely a different sector of the field.

10.

Economists have not learned that politics is made of language.

“Natural resources” are bones.

11.

“Epic fail”; “novel fail”; “aphorism fail.”

Like when an ant loses control of its mandible
and drops the torso of a wasp.

12.

Resentment is the dried blood of wounded virtue.

The Utah of emotions.

13.

Would you like to know my secrets?
I don’t have any.
My secrets are feelings.
I have a secret, but I don’t know what it is yet.

14.

In the early 70s Hannah Arendt warned against routine crimes of government.

On *House of Cards*, a show about routine crimes of government, a man lies, kills, becomes president.

Arendt also warned, in the 60s, against the fatal stupidity of the powerful.

On *Orange Is the New Black*, an incarcerated mother tells her incarcerated daughter,

“Lots of stupid people go on to become great successes.”

15.

It’s hard to think if you’re always getting interrupted.
If your status is: “Interruptible.”

Surveillance is nothing new.

The child hangs an aspiration on the door:

Private

Do Not Enter

16.

Remember Virginia Woolf's little silvery fish of thought?
It starts to glimmer forth but abruptly disappears
when her protagonist is interrupted by the Beadle
enforcing spatial prohibitions on thought.

If to wander in solitude subjects you to violence

you have been disinvited from thought

and there is no such thing, for you, as a republic.

17.

Milan Kundera wrote

Totalitarian society, especially in its more extreme versions, tends to abolish the boundary between the public and the private; power, as it grows ever more opaque, requires the lives of its citizens to be entirely transparent. The ideal of life without secrets *corresponds to the ideal of the exemplary family: a citizen does not have the right to hide anything at all from the Party or the State, just as a child has no right to keep a secret from his father or his mother.*

In their propaganda, totalitarian societies project an idyllic smile: they want to be seen as "one big family."

18.

Walking on eggshells in a forest.
Don't want to wake up the trees, or kill them.

Seeing a bird you've never seen and having a sinking feeling: what if it's the last one?

Worrying about nature, like holding a sick infant in the Newborn Intensive Care Unit.
"Maybe my love will make a difference."
"That's not falsifiable."

Babies thrive when they are loved.

Is nature similar?

Am I projecting on nature, or am I nature?

Am I history's ventriloquist or nature's dummy?

Philippe Descola wrote

Between the effacement of humans
in the virginity of a practical world
without rules or representations
and the preponderance of the human
in the definition of that which makes sense on the earth,
the middle path of being-in-the-world
lurches through numerous zigzags.

19.

Who isn't a stranger?

The feelings of others are enigmatic and soldiers are young.

"You killed people!"

"Nobody told me they were real."

What if the norm was to send the white bourgeoisie to war?

"Come on, let's not kill ourselves here. Life's too short!"

He rubs his elbows.

"Where can I find a decent cappuccino?"

20.

Paul Celan wrote

If I were like you. If you were like me.
Did we not stand
under one *trade wind?*
We are strangers.

21.

In Errol Morris's documentary about him, *The Unknown Known,* Donald Rumsfeld exclaimed, "It would have been *wonderful* if we had killed Saddam Hussein at Dora Farms!"

"I'll have the pie à la mode."

"*Wonderful*!"

Allen Ginsberg said

Almost all our language has been taxed by war.

Errol Morris's last question: "Why are you talking to me?"

Rumsfeld answers, "That's a *vicious* question . . . I don't know."

Known, unknown . . .

Extemporizing, ad-libbing: it doesn't always end well.

iMouth.

"Did I really just say that?"

Hart Crane wrote

The phonographs of hades in the brain
Are tunnels that rewind themselves.

22.

Knowing the answers in advance, that's ideology.
Hold the future still.

Ignore contradiction,

like an unwanted chore.

Don't look back,
don't look down
into the roots of things.

Jacques Rancière wrote

The indeterminate ritual of demystification continues to impose a way of thinking (and practicing) democracy on the basis of suspicion, as if it always had to be made to confess that it is not what it claims to be, and that those who practice it are perpetually deluded about what they are doing.

Suspicious of paranoia.

Or when justice also means holding words accountable.

23.

The wall at the 24 Divisadero bus stop

on Divisadero and Haight

used to say

the future is passé.

24.

In the early 1960s, when a bill against
gender discrimination
would come before the Senate,
it was considered hilarious.
The bill would come up.
The mood would turn jocular.
One senator joked, “When I argue with my wife,
I always get the last two words: yes, dear.”

Multiple-choice quiz: what is the correct way to gloss this period piece?

a) Power pretends to fake it.
b) Heteronormative comedy revolves around the failure to collaborate.
c) Because we all know whose acquiescence is no joke
d) Because we all know who really fakes it

25.

Silent meditation—it looks grim but it's fun.
Party—it looks fun but it's grim.

26.

If *you* hit on you, would you want yourself?
Would you know exactly what to say?
Would you confidently seduce yourself?

Or would you be like,

"Look, I'm not a mind reader."

"Fuck it, this is too much work."

27.

I opened my mouth and millions of bees flew out.
    I closed my mouth; my body filled with smoke.
I opened my mouth and millions of bees flew out.
    I closed my mouth; my body filled with water.
I opened my mouth and millions of bees flew out.
    I closed my mouth; my body filled with hands.
I opened my mouth and millions of bees flew out.
    I closed my mouth; my body filled with tiny
    trampolines.
I opened my mouth and millions of bees flew out.
    I closed my mouth; my body filled with other
    people's bad memories.
I opened my mouth and millions of bees flew out.
    I closed my mouth; my body filled with dead bees.
I opened my mouth and nothing came out.

To lay our grievances at their feet now would be unkind. They are almost done doing their peculiar damage. We can take a little more. We are the kings of evasion, while they are about to lie down and die.

But then they don't die.

Perhaps if we do speak, they will die?

Perhaps that is why we don't speak.

28.

Our next-door neighbor is in the Special Forces. “Don’t worry,” he says, “I’ve turned off my web monitoring, I’m not monitoring the websites you visit.”

I am stuck in a pause.

Liliana Lukin wrote

there is a silence here

that has nothing to do with silence.

Rae Armantrout wrote

Find the place
in silence
that is a person

or like a person
or like not
needing a person

29.

Phobias:
Surveillance
Narcissists
People whose legend precedes them
Show trials
Indoor parking lots
Off-gassing
Predators
Bleach
Drones
Self-righteousness
Subtlety
Lack of subtlety

Liliana Mizrahi wrote

I am, for myself, a hypothesis . . .

Osvaldo Lamborghini said

I said no to the mirror

30.

With soil depletion due to capitalist genetics, food becomes representation, just a chewy sign. “Food” becomes the epitaph for food, nutrients an extinct language, lost in translation.

“If everyone has their basic needs met, I’ll lose business.”

But time is not a fish,
waiting to be caught.

31.

Mahmoud Darwish wrote

The myths refuse to adjust their plot.
They may suffer a sudden malfunction
and some of the ships may drift to a dry
unpopulated land
where the imaginary becomes afflicted with the real . . .

32.

Sometimes you arbitrarily encounter a piece of writing
that makes you feel, "*This* is the key to my
whole existence."

It makes sense that someone's mind gave you access
to yours.
Someone else's body gave you your body, too.

But about this reading that has unlocked you?
What if you had never come across it?
Why does it happen repeatedly,
with really different writings?
How many such "keys" are there
to your whole existence?
Three? Ninety? Seven thousand? Countless?

33.

Can I see that which I am outside of?
Can I see that which I am not outside of?

Amieka wrote

I'm going to draw a line straight through it

34.

In the future, they had speculative temperaments.

Speaking languages and practicing art forms was entertainment.

Is there music on Mars?
Do androids dream of electric sheep?
What was it about the subjective mind
that made it feel so private?

Our minds are always ready to render the world into experience.

What other kind of mind might there be?

Could objectivity reach across to other worlds

if the facts of other worlds

and the facts of ours were not shared?

What logic would form the basis of our commonality,
the logic of concepts, abstractions, numbers, dreams?

Could worlds made of dreaming exist and how could
we discover them?

When all of the world's problems were solved,
we became cosmologists.

35.

"The spirit is willing."
What about the flesh?
"The flesh is too."
How about history?

History has no plan.

36.

We have a fight about
. . . ferns.

A bee angrily chases me away from the lavender.

I fall: break nothing.

That's my run-in with the law

of nature, today.

37.

Vulnerability
a timeless antique.

38.

Your silence feels vindictive.
Maybe you are just busy? Busy feeling hostile.

You're angry because I've understood you.
You're angry because I've misunderstood you.

Your revenge will be to make yourself too important to reply.

But it won't work; I've known you too long.
That is to say, you're already too important to me.

Your new importance means nothing to the ones who love you best.

39.

“Dear” “pro-lifers”:

You’ve mistaken your atavistic fantasy for historical necessity.

Your perceptions are metaphors; your metaphors are symptoms.

A rudimentary dose of empiricism would be transformative for you.

Your discourse is a landfill disguised as nature.

Your edifice crumbles on a sinking island.

Self-criticism is preferable to ideology.

Try, as Paul Celan put it

two

mouthfuls of silence

D.W. Winnicott wrote

It appalls me to think how much deep change I have
prevented or delayed by my personal need to interpret.

40.

Kurt Gray wrote

In the bright light of moral condemnation,
harm is a ubiquitous shadow.
If you can't see it from where you're standing,
just shift your perspective.

The shoes of self-righteousness are tight.
You have to take them off sometimes.

41.

The circle of fifths is a dictionary of all keys.
Demystifications is a key ring: a circle of keys.
Remember making mobiles with old keys?
Hanging them from hangers?

42.

Do you know the word *dialogue*?
How about *conversation*?

It's not the same as *monologue*,
where one person talks the whole time.

43.

Not antisocial.

Gregarious—with faeries.

44.

I'll take my small talk dry.

45.

To show that an idea has a history in order to reclaim it.

To show that an idea has a history in order to debunk it.

History: exhibiting rationales.

46.

Brian Teare wrote

illness keeps
a little calendar

Nietzsche wrote

For there is no health as such, and all attempts to define a thing that way have been wretched failures.

47.

Robert Kocik wrote

An architecture based on the stress response would, above all, dispel the delusion that individual and collective interests are at odds—a dichotomy responsible for the greater part of our wretchedness.

Levi R. Bryant wrote

. . . political questions of emancipation and resistance are . . . intimately related to questions of social time and space, and the question of the political becomes that of how we might achieve speeds required for attaining escape velocity with respect to oppressive gravitational fields or social assemblages . . .

When militarized borders, fences, and walls had been
torn down,
turned to sculpture,
when the seas had been restored to the right alkalinity,

fish returned,

when the skies were full of birds again,

forests with animals,

when the rains fell in their turn,

icepack back,

when everyone had medicine, food, housing, gardens,
tools, and schools,

prisons closed,

and the wars had all ended,

all feeling beings

across time and space

experienced knowledge

as a collective organ.

48.

Quoting Walter Benjamin, Susan Buck-Morss wrote

Wish images "innervate" the "technical organ of the collective," supplying it with nerve stimulation that prompts revolutionary action—"like the child who learns [the practical task of] grasping by trying [impossibly] to catch the moon in its hands."

49.

Though we should not take our perceptions too literally—we should remember that perception is always relative—what we perceive together dissolves us into connection.

We meet at a vanishing point of perspective, converge into shared understanding and its object.

The world, the moon, and the sun are round.
We all know that roundness,
and all of the dead have known it.
This brings the living and the dead together.
We are that which transpires and it's not nothing to
know that, and the planet's roundness,
its many rocks, a thin sliver of shared atmosphere,
though who knows what air means,
apart from breathing.

In a hundred years, we will all have been "replaced."

Léopold Sédar Senghor wrote

And even his song, the melody and rhythm of his song
are dictated to him.

50.

After hearing *Demystifications* #1–45
at a Midwestern university
a man comes close and asks
must ideology critique now come in the form of memes?

Is ideology critique becoming stupefied?

This was a man whose legend preceded him
(see *Demystification* #29)
by about two feet.

One heard his rhetorical question
well before his mouth opened (see *Demystification* #2).

51.

A head on your right is turned towards you.
A purgatorial mouth is moving
towards the reply of your eye,
the acquiescence of your ear.

It says anything; it can't go on,
it must go on.

It speaks to what, of what,
on what, toward what, about what?

52.

Politeness is the price you pay

for not wanting what is offered.

53.

She paused to see if she could sense the time-being

and heard the low rumble of the planet turning.

54.

Who regales the world
on the topic of individual freedom
having stolen everything
even that concept.

55.

Etel Adnan wrote

We are never alone because of the way memory functions.

What about history?
What is the difference between history and memory?

We are never alone because of the way history functions.

56.

Whereas all the other trails on the map are irregular,
miles long, meandering,
Tuur's hypothetical Artist's Trail is very small,
a perfectly geometrical circle.

We entertain the idea of Bureaucrat's Trail in a straight
line; where would it go?
"Straight off the cliff," he proposes.

For some years Revital and Tuur could not arrange
the shipping of the albino goldfish they conceived.

"But you became artists to avoid bureaucracy?"
"*No*! Bureaucracy *is* our medium."

A sculptor a few chairs and plates down wonders
to the person next to her:

"The rents are so high in the cities.
Where are artists supposed to live?"

57.

What is the social command?

Who hears it, and what do they hear?

It was the first time he had been to the sea.

He made a sculpture using only materials he found there.

Then Blessing Ngobeni said

This is a sculpture of the sea listening to itself.

The burden of the past
weighs heavy on his heart.

"History is best forgotten," he says,
gesturing with his hand.
"I paint for the future."

Marx wrote

. . . the social revolution . . .

cannot create its poetry out of the past,

but only from the future.

. . . let the dead bury the dead.

But history is not so easily forgotten
It has a way of coming back
Sadness itself.

Susan Buck-Morss wrote of the "dialectic that makes possible the transition to a socialist society"

. . . if future history is not determined and thus its forms are still unknown, if consciousness cannot transcend the horizons of its sociohistorical context, then where else but to the dead past can imagination turn in order to conceptualize a world that is "not-yet"? Moreover,

such a move itself satisfies a utopian wish: the desire (manifested in the religious myth of awakening the dead) "to make suffering into something incomplete," to make good an unfulfilled past that has been irretrievably lost.

On another occasion he wore a cow's head
stripped of its skin
to an art gallery
in Johannesburg.

He wanted to know,
once the cow's head was on his,
if the other gallery visitors
would appear to be human or
cow?

And what will be the basis, he asked,
for racist discrimination
when I am thus masked?

58.

Cassie has had an astrological chart done
for the credit rating system
which was originated by an abolitionist;

apparently the credit rating system's
Chiron is in Cancer.

Her alternative credit rating agency grants you credence

by asking

What is your real story?

59.

key cud wire trachea rug catechism

tension rib mesh druid kin brain

data hole, hard pericardium, ever's metatarsal

60.

The Infant does not speak
but survives

received
bathed, rocked, and named

Will itself.

61.

For Muriel Rukeyser to grow meant to move past
false barriers

She wrote that
the drives of poetry and science share in

open-endedness over the fatal telos
of instrumentality

She wrote that

the world of the poet
is the scientist's world. Their claim on systems
is the same claim.
Their writings anticipate each other;
welcome each other;
indeed embrace

Poets and scientists give themselves closely
to the creation and description of systems

It is not a matter of using the results of science,
but of seeing that there is a meeting place between
all kinds of imagination

Poetry can provide that meeting place

62.

A crystal, like a person, has facets.
A face
is a facet of what?

Emmanuel Lévinas wrote

The face says do not kill me

63.

Walter Benjamin wrote

What matters here is that the face of the world, the colossal head, precisely in what is newest never itself changes—that this "newest" remains in all respects the same. This constitutes the eternity of hell and the sadist's delight in innovation. To determine the totality of traits which define this "modernity" is to represent hell.

64.

Staretz Silouan wrote

Keep your mind in hell,
and despair not.

65.

The happy

are kin. And the sad.

Our feelings are sisters.

Sometimes your feeling is my great-grandmother

and mine is your second cousin, once removed.

66.

An argument.

One attacks another for knowing only one language.

"*Monolingual!*"

A curse: *you one tongue!*

"I had responsibilities growing up; we were poor.
I went to bad public schools. My single mother worked."

Excuses, excuses.

"What about my fluency in the language of survival?"

Lazy.

But what if there is no such thing as laziness?

Porpentine wrote

Laziness is not laziness, it is many things: avoiding encountering one's own body, avoiding triggers, avoiding thinking about the future because it's proven to be unbearable.

Jacques Rancière wrote

The master is always a length ahead of the student, who always feels that in order to go farther he must have another master, supplementary explications. Thus does the triumphant Achilles drag Hector's corpse, attached to his chariot, around the city of Troy. Reasoned progress of knowledge is an indefinitely reproduced mutilation. . . . Don't ask if the little educated child suffers from this mutilation. The system's genius is to transform loss into profit. The child advances. *He has been taught, therefore he has learned, therefore he can forget. Behind him the abyss of ignorance is being dug again. But here's the amazing part: from now on the ignorance is someone else's.*

Silvan Tomkins wrote

How does interest support the necessary and the possible?

There is no human competence which can be achieved in the absence of a sustaining interest, and the development of cognitive competence is peculiarly vulnerable to anomie.

67.

The good-enough mother.

The golden child.

A poet with a PhD has a child about to be "school-age." Unlike most parents in her demographic, she doesn't try to get him into "the best school." She doesn't put him on waiting lists or enter him into lotteries. She will send him, she says, to the local public school down the street.

"I want him to be mediocre," she says.

From *medius,* "middle" + *ocris*, "jagged mountain," cognate with Greek *okris*, "peak, point," Welsh *ochr*, "corner, border," Latin *acer*, "sharp."

Prior to the sixteenth century, another name for the Golden Mean was *Golden Mediocrity*.

The golden mother.

The good-enough child.

Donato said

Culture is ordinary . . .

68.

What about being taught to desire something you don't really want?

Time-honored radical solutions:

1) Denigrate and insult what is widely touted as desirable (marriage; property; procreation; the gratuitous thing hermetically bound in thick plastics; the admiration of the hapless; a Grand Prize, yet another whatever, and so on).

2) A character can want, and even achieve, things on your behalf (reunions with the dead; chimera-love), putting desire at an angle, freeing you to want otherwise.

Dorothea Casaubon wrote

"I try not to have desires merely for myself . . .".

69.

Virginia Woolf wrote

In the vast catastrophe of the European war our emotions had to be broken up for us, and put at an angle from us, before we could allow ourselves to feel them . . .

70.

Politics _____ facts:

a) can't keep up with
b) would prefer to ignore
c) are worried about
d) don't understand

Facts _____ aesthetics:

a) can't keep up with
b) would prefer to ignore
c) are worried about
d) don't understand

Aesthetics _____ politics:

a) can't keep up with
b) would prefer to ignore
c) are worried about
d) don't understand

All antagonisms precede and await us.

71.

Pseudofact Is Over! (If You Want It.)

72.

John Berger wrote

The living are the core of the dead.

73.

Walter Benjamin wrote

The last journey of the flâneur: Death.

74.

Charlotte Joko Beck wrote

Suppose I'm condemned to have my head chopped off in a guillotine. Now I'm being marched up the steps onto the platform. Can I maintain attention to the moment? Can I be aware of each step, step-by-step? Can I place my head in the guillotine carefully so that I serve the executioner well?

75.

The commodity is
"human labor in the abstract."

Appearing seamless it seems   to lack sediment
as if it emanated   as miracle
from its point of sale

76.

Lucien wrote

Holes are not traps, are not compliant, have no telos.
Holes are made of tiny holes.

77.

Perhaps every detail of your life
conscious and unconscious
has already been written.

Not the personality's version of it.

78.

The forgiveness cloak,

green and thick,

one size fits all.

79.

Order and sensitivity are somatic matters.
Certain days, tiredness spreads limitlessly.
Details recede and disappear.
Cause and effect fall down.
The tides turn
against each other.

80.

Jeroen Mettes wrote

Composition is not design, but the production of an
autonomous block of affects . . .
rhythmically subtracted from the language of
a community.

81.

Rolf Tiedemann wrote

For the early Surrealists, both dream and reality would unravel to a dreamed, unreal Reality, from which no way led back to contemporary praxis and its demands.

Brian Massumi wrote

Context is a general concept . . . animal politics resists the pieties of context.

Gilles Deleuze wrote

The writer returns from what he has seen and heard with bloodshot eyes and pierced eardrums.

82.

Roxy wrote

No one has respect for original art.

She wants repair visible, not to hide the break, to see the fissure in the fix.

83.

Steph intends to

excavate that which appears to be already above ground.

84.

You could deliberately do things wrong.

Louis Aragon wrote

And, like most of my friends, I was partial to failures, to what is monstrous and cannot survive, cannot succeed. . . . I was like them: I preferred error to its opposite.

85.

Clare intends to

use poetic knowledge to make myself untouchable.

86.

Some magnet pulls; small filings aggregate into a shape: mother, God, justice, truth. What is the relationship between the nameless thing that pulls and the named thing we chase? If we attend only to the action of the pull . . . and ignore the "magnet" . . .

87.

Trending on Google today:

Snake, hummingbird, spider, Pluto, hallelujah, and *Adderall.*

A relationship advice site says: "If you're feeling disconnected from your partner, spend time together comparing your relationship to other relationships worse than yours. This will bring you closer."

88.

Jean-Luc Nancy wrote

No culture has lived as our modern culture has in the endless accumulation of archives and expectations.

No culture has made present the past and the future to the point of removing the present from its own passage.

89.

At five- and ten-second intervals conceptions are turned on the lathe of commodification: thought package. How deep runs the error of unceasing production.

90.

About those who would seem "to know too much too soon," Kathi Weeks cautions

. . . there are advantages, I claim, to more partial visions of alternatives, fragments or glimpses of something different that do not presume to add up to a blueprint of an already named future with a preconceived content.

91.

Cognition, the ignited cog—is all thinking in part magical thinking?

Jean-Luc Nancy wrote

I am speaking of a present in which something or someone presents itself: the present of an arrival, an approach . . . adoration, directed at singularity as such . . . the singular, and its singular way to come into presence—flower, face, or tone . . . something inestimable . . . so exceeding any possible calculation that one does not even try to imagine it.

92.

Tiny activations as homeopathic antidotes to over-action's calamities: milk thistle/plutonium; oyster mushroom/crude oil; assemble on the tracks/coal train–blockade/undo.

Claudia Rankine wrote

That's the bruise the ice in the heart was meant to ice

93.

When I was small my mother told me,
"Money doesn't grow on trees."
Later I told my sister the news: "Money grows on trees!"

We ran outside to check the spindly, hard-pressed tree
growing in front of our apartment on Clayton Street.

A packet of food stamps lay on the sidewalk, near the tree.

We picked it up and opened it.

It was empty, all the food stamps torn out.

Adorno wrote

An exaggeration which no longer measures itself against something given or presupposed, something to which it could be reduced and which would account for its intelligibility is neither an indication of truth nor a symptom of madness and delusion, it is neither thinking nor its opposite, rather it is thinking as gesture.

94.

“Mandala”

. . . was an important word for my mother. Also

“opportunist”—an insult. And “martyr”—

Don’t complain.
Don’t be a martyr.
Real martyrs don’t complain.

Displacement
a red shift.

The revolutionary, large as history, always in the break.

95.

reckon | complain

strategic | pure

give | calculate

forgive | accuse

breathe | consume

help | exclude

balm | burn

listen | rationalize

apologize | justify

humility | sanctimony

recuse | comply

confront | pacify

argue | pretend

make | buy

feel | medicate

apologize | blame

reciprocate | ignore

Simone Weil wrote

Contradiction is the criterion of the real.

96.

Not To-Do List:

Not to fail to help
Not to claim exception
Not to forget how to speak
in case they ever stop talking

Frank O'Hara wrote

run your finger along your no-moss mind
that's not a thought that's soot

97.

Biodiversity—a 'communism of nonequivalence.'

Jean-Luc Nancy wrote

Equality is not that equivalence of individuals of which the idea of "democracy" makes us think first of all—favoring thus insidiously both mercantile equivalence and the atomization of "subjects," each as catastrophic as the other. Quite the opposite, "democracy" should be thought of starting only from the equality of incommensurables: absolute and irreducible singulars that are not individuals or social groups but sudden appearances, arrivals and departures, voices, tones—here and now, every instant. To demand equality for tomorrow is first of all to assert it today, and by the same gesture to reject catastrophic equivalence. It is to assert common equality, common incommensurability: a communism of nonequivalence.

Each as catastrophic as the other.

98.

Another idea for a TV show, it's called *Office Hours*. Every episode someone different coming to office hours.

99.

Fanny Howe wrote

The person actually knows the planet and the cosmos better than she knows her own self that disappears.

Edward Said wrote

Regard all experiences as if they were about to disappear.

ACKNOWLEDGMENTS & CREDITS

Many thanks go to the Headlands Center for the Arts where *Demystifications* was first conceived. To the authors, friends, and students cited and sighted in the constellation that is this book I extend my appreciation, respect, and admiration. And to Eirik Steinhoff—as ever.

Rae Armantrout, excerpt from "A Pulse," *Veil: New and Selected Poems*, Middletown: Wesleyan University Press, 2001; Paul Celan, "Language Mesh" from *Speech-Grille and Selected Poems*, translated by Joachim Neugroschel, New York: Dutton, 1971; Liliana Lukin, *Descomposición*, Ediciones de la Flor, S.R.L., 1986; Jean-Luc Nancy, *After Fukushima: The Equivalence of Catastrophes*, translated by Charlotte Mandell, New York: Fordham University Press, 2014; Frank O'Hara, excerpt from "Song (Is it dirty)" from *Lunch Poems*. Copyright © 1964, 2014 by Maureen O'Hara, Administratrix of the Estate of Frank O'Hara. Reprinted with the permission of The Permissions Company, Inc., on behalf of City Lights Books, www.citylights.com; Kathi Weeks, *The Problem with Work: Feminism, Marxism, Antiwork Politics, and Postwork Imaginaries*, Durham: Duke University Press, 2011.

Other titles by MIRANDA MELLIS include *The Revisionist, The Spokes, None of This Is Real, The Quarry,* and *Materialisms*. She coauthored *The Instead* with Emily Abendroth and coedited *The Encyclopedia Project*. She lives in the Pacific Northwest and teaches at The Evergreen State College.